Original title:
Love's Leverage

Copyright © 2024 Swan Charm
All rights reserved.

Author: Sara Säde
ISBN HARDBACK: 978-9916-86-566-8
ISBN PAPERBACK: 978-9916-86-567-5
ISBN EBOOK: 978-9916-86-568-2

Exchanges of Essence

In the quiet whispers shared,
Two souls entwined in grace,
Secrets of the heart laid bare,
A dance of time and space.

Electric pulses gently flow,
In every glance, a spark is found,
Words enrich what feelings grow,
In silence, hearts beat sound.

Moments weave a tapestry,
Of laughter, tears, and sighs,
Understanding's harmony,
Where truth and love arise.

Through storms and gentle winds they sail,
Navigating dreams anew,
Learning from each tender tale,
In each, a part of true.

Beneath the stars, they make a vow,
To honor what they've shared,
In every breath, a promise now,
A bond throughout declared.

A Precision of Passion

In moments fleeting, eyes collide,
Messages without a sound,
Feelings coursing like a tide,
In every heartbeat, profound.

Carefully crafted words dance free,
A symphony of tender grace,
Each note a shared intimacy,
In every touch, the space.

Sculpting time like softest clay,
A masterpiece of souls entwined,
Guided by a gentle sway,
Where body, heart, and mind.

With ardor, the canvas burns bright,
Colors splash in splendor bold,
Each brushstroke captures the light,
In passion, stories unfold.

In every glance, a truth revealed,
A promise in the silent night,
With fervor, all wounds are healed,
In love's exquisite flight.

The Equilibrium of Feelings

In the scales where hearts reside,
Balancing joy and pain,
Harmony where love can bide,
In sunshine and in rain.

Gentle tides, they rise and fall,
In every pulse, a measured beat,
Trusting in the silent call,
Completeness in the sweet.

Through valleys deep, we navigate,
A journey fraught with bends,
In patience, we articulate,
What every heartbeat sends.

Colors of emotions blend,
A spectrum vast and wide,
Finding solace, hand in hand,
In truth, we shall abide.

In the stillness, there's a space,
Where vulnerabilities bloom,
In between, we find our place,
A love that chases gloom.

The Influence of Mutual Dreams

In twilight's hush, we dare to dream,
With visions shared, we rise,
Bound by the silver moonbeam,
Crafting futures with our eyes.

With every wish, a path unfolds,
Echoes of our hearts align,
In the tapestry, stories told,
Where souls meet, intertwine.

Together we chase the dawn's light,
Shaping skies with whispered schemes,
In the depths of the night,
Our hearts forge the wildest dreams.

A landscape filled with hope anew,
Each step a dance with fate,
In mirroring worlds, we view,
Time bends and we create.

United in a sacred trust,
In dreams, we find our way,
With every heartbeat, pure and just,
Love's influence shall stay.

The Balance of Belonging

In shadows cast, we find our place,
Where echoes of laughter start to race.
Hearts entwined, in silent song,
A dance of souls where we belong.

Through trials faced, we weave our thread,
In moments cherished, fears are shed.
Together strong, we brave the night,
In bonds of trust, we find our light.

Amid the chaos, we stand tall,
In love's embrace, we never fall.
The ties we forge, a map to guide,
Through all of life's relentless tide.

With every heartbeat, whispers near,
A language shared, so pure, so clear.
In harmony, we share our dreams,
In unity, we find our seams.

So let us cherish this sacred bond,
Through changing tides, our hearts respond.
In every moment, we choose to stay,
Together we rise, come what may.

Anchored Aspirations

Beneath the stars, our dreams ignite,
With steadfast hearts, we chase the light.
In winds of change, we find our way,
With courage strong, we seize the day.

Each wave that crashes brings us near,
In oceans vast, we have no fear.
Together bound, we chart our course,
In every challenge, we find our force.

With whispered hopes, we lift our sails,
Through tempests fierce and gentle gales.
In unity, our spirits soar,
In every heartbeat, we want more.

Anchored deep in love's embrace,
We traverse time, we find our space.
With every dusk, new dawns arise,
In shared ambitions, we'll touch the skies.

So let us dream, let courage flow,
In every moment, let love grow.
With hands held tight, we face the strife,
Together we weave our tapestry of life.

Eloquent Gravity

In silent force, connection feels,
A pull so strong, it softly heals.
With every glance, a thread we weave,
In quiet moments, we believe.

Through realms unknown, we navigate,
In gentle tides, we oscillate.
With every step, a dance so rare,
In the weight of love, we find our care.

Like stars aligned in cosmic dance,
In unison, we take the chance.
With gravity's touch, our spirits rise,
In depths of truth, we realize.

An eloquence in being near,
In every heartbeat, echoes clear.
Through whispered dreams and softest sighs,
We find our home in each other's eyes.

So let us drift in harmony,
In gravity, we find our free.
With tethered hearts and open minds,
In love's embrace, true peace we find.

Threads of Companionship

In woven paths, our stories blend,
Each thread a promise, each knot a friend.
Through laughter shared and tears we shed,
In every moment, love is spread.

With gentle hands, we braid our days,
In vibrant hues, we paint our ways.
Through every storm, we find our grace,
In threads of trust, a warm embrace.

With every memory, we stitch anew,
In patterns rich, our friendship grew.
Amidst the noise, we find our song,
Through every challenge, we stand strong.

In shared adventures, we laugh and roam,
In every step, we feel at home.
With whispered dreams and secrets shared,
In threads of love, we are ensnared.

So let us cherish this bond so bright,
In every dawn, and every night.
With threads of companionship, we bind,
In every heartbeat, our hearts aligned.

Embracing Gravity

In the quiet fall of night,
We find our way through stars,
With every weight we carry,
We learn just who we are.

Pulling close the dreams we chase,
Lifting hearts, grounding fears,
Together we can break the space,
And wipe away the tears.

Each moment brings its tether,
Binding souls with sacred trust,
Finding strength in every feather,
As we rise from earth to dust.

In this dance of give and take,
We share the weight, the grace,
Hand in hand, we never break,
In our own timeless place.

So let the universe conspire,
With each heavy breath we share,
In gravity we find our fire,
A love beyond compare.

Bonds of Tenderness

In the cradle of your arms,
Lies a warmth I can believe,
Every touch a gentle charm,
In this bond, we find reprieve.

Soft whispers in the dark,
Carve our secrets in the night,
With every heartbeat, every spark,
We radiate the purest light.

Though the world may not yet see,
What our hearts can truly know,
In silence, our souls are free,
Together, we will always grow.

Every glance a tender vow,
In the chaos, we're the calm,
Here and now, we take this bow,
Wrapped in love, a healing balm.

So I hold you close and tight,
In the stillness, we are one,
Bonds of tenderness take flight,
Until our days are done.

The Pressure of Passion

Underneath the blazing sun,
We ignite the restless flame,
With your kiss, my heart's begun,
In this dance, we play the game.

Turbulence in every breath,
As we climb the hills of fate,
What we feel is life and death,
In your arms, I gravitate.

Rushing tides of sweet desire,
Carving moments in the sand,
With each heartbeat, dreams conspire,
We burn brightly, hand in hand.

Through the chaos, we hold fast,
Like the stars, we bend and break,
In this pressure, love will last,
With each treasure that we make.

So let's embrace this wild ride,
With every passion-filled embrace,
Side by side, let worlds collide,
In the beauty of our space.

Sacred Exchange

In the silence, we connect,
Hearts unveiled, a gentle grace,
Through our words, we can reflect,
In this sacred, timeless place.

Every glance a quiet promise,
In the warmth of shared delight,
What we find, no one can harness,
In the softness of the night.

Through the laughter and the tears,
We entwine our souls so bold,
With each step, we face our fears,
In this journey, love unfolds.

With the passing of each hour,
We learn the art of giving,
In our hands, we hold the power,
In this bond, we find our living.

So let our hearts beat as one,
In the rhythm of exchange,
Together, we have just begun,
In a love that feels so strange.

Tender Returns

In the hush of evening light,
Shadows dance, hearts take flight.
Whispers float on soft, cool air,
Promises held with gentle care.

Echoes of laughter grace the night,
Memories bloom, a pure delight.
Stars awaken, a twinkling sight,
In their glow, we find what's right.

Time weaves threads, both old and new,
Each moment shared feels like a clue.
The warmth of love, a sweet embrace,
Together we find our rightful place.

Waves of joy crash on the shore,
Each tide whispers, we crave more.
With every touch, our spirits soar,
In tender returns, we restore.

Through the seasons, we grow and change,
In the dance of life, we rearrange.
Hand in hand, we face the fray,
In love's journey, we've found our way.

The Cost of Connection

In the silence, hearts collide,
Vulnerability, we cannot hide.
A whispered truth, a secret shared,
Yet with it comes the weight we bared.

Each bond forged is not for free,
Trust and fear, a tangled spree.
We risk the pain to feel the thrill,
In the dance of connection, time stands still.

Every tear shed, a price we pay,
For the love that brightens our day.
Yet the ache teaches us to grow,
In every heartbeat, we come to know.

Fragile threads weave us tight,
In the darkness, we seek the light.
To connect is to dive and plunge,
In vulnerability, we learn to lunge.

Though costs may mount, the riches gleam,
In each connection, we find the dream.
Through every struggle, every scar,
The value lies in who we are.

Sway of Silent Longing

In twilight's glow, shadows play,
A silent longing leads the way.
Moments pass, yet time stands still,
In the heart, a quiet thrill.

Gentle breezes beckon near,
Carrying whispers that we hear.
In the stillness, hope ignites,
Swaying softly through endless nights.

Every glance, a hero's call,
Echoes of love in every hall.
With each heartbeat, the silence sings,
A world of dreams that longing brings.

The dance of wishes in the dark,
Unspoken truths leave their mark.
In secret breaths, our spirits soar,
A yearning deep we can't ignore.

In the distance, shadows glide,
Two souls entwined, no need to hide.
For in the silence, love will bloom,
A bright light chasing away the gloom.

The Value Found in Togetherness

In the warmth of shared delight,
We find our strength, a guiding light.
Laughter echoes, hearts align,
In togetherness, the stars combine.

Through storms and trials, side by side,
In every tear, we learn to ride.
Each moment stitched, a tapestry,
The threads of love, our legacy.

In quiet corners, stories told,
Generations weave, both fierce and bold.
The value blooms, with roots that bind,
In the garden of hearts intertwined.

With hands held tight, we face the night,
In your gaze, the world feels right.
In every stride, a rhythm flows,
Together, the spirit of love grows.

As seasons change and years reveal,
In togetherness, we learn to heal.
The treasure of hearts in open homes,
In the love shared, no one roams.

Bridges of the Heart

With gentle whispers, we pave the way,
Constructing moments in joyful play.
These bridges span the great divide,
In love's embrace, we shall abide.

Steadying Forces

Through darkest nights, your light will guide,
In love's embrace, we shall abide.
You are my force, my solid ground,
In your arms, my peace is found.

Unraveled Threads

Through joy and sorrow, we sew anew,
With every fiber, our hearts imbue.
Unraveled, yet whole, we find our bliss,
In harmony's song, we seal our kiss.

The Lyric of Affection

Together we rise, with voices clear,
In the lyric of affection dear.
In every breath, our love proclaimed,
With passion's fire, forever flamed.

In the Shadow of Devotion

In the quiet hush of night,
Hearts whisper each gentle plight.
Promises linger in soft glow,
In the shadow where love does grow.

Through trials faced, side by side,
A bond unbreakable, a steadfast guide.
Every tear and every smile,
Etched in time, we'll walk each mile.

Golden moments framed in grace,
In the shadow, we find our place.
Hands entwined, we touch the sky,
In devotion, we learn to fly.

With every heartbeat, a silent vow,
Together we rise, we take our bow.
Through storm and calm, our spirits soar,
In the shadow of love, forevermore.

The Trade Winds of Desire

Whispers carried on the breeze,
Sailing hearts with effortless ease.
Chasing dreams through sunlit skies,
In the trade winds, passion flies.

Sparkling stars, they light the way,
Guiding souls where hearts will sway.
With every gust, new journeys bloom,
In desire's dance, there is no gloom.

Tides of yearning ebb and flow,
In soft caress, the feelings grow.
Across the waves, our love will glide,
In the trade winds, side by side.

Moments stolen, hearts entwined,
In these currents, forever blind.
Desire's flame will never wane,
In the trade winds, we'll sustain.

Stakes of the Soul

Beneath the weight of silent fears,
Lies the essence of all our years.
Each moment's choice, a sacred toll,
Where we gamble the stakes of the soul.

With every heartbeat, a risk we take,
In the shadows, we bend, we break.
Rising high, only to fall,
In this game, we risk it all.

Connections forged in fiery pain,
From fragile loss, our joys regain.
Through sacrifice, we emerge whole,
Navigating the stakes of the soul.

In laughter's glow or sorrow's chime,
Each step we take, a dance with time.
With courage fierce, we accept the role,
In this fragile world, the stakes of the soul.

The Scale of Sentiments

On a delicate balance, feelings sway,
Each emotion held in disarray.
From joy to sorrow, love to strife,
Measured gently, the weight of life.

Kindness beckons with gentle hands,
While bitterness shifts like shifting sands.
In this scale, we find our place,
Crafting harmony with every trace.

Through laughter's echo and silence deep,
In the heart's rhythm, our secrets keep.
What we cherish, what we regret,
In this scale, our truths are set.

Embracing all that we hold dear,
In the scale of sentiments, crystal clear.
Life's tapestry, woven tight,
In every shade, we find our light.

The Echo of Us

In the shadows where whispers dwell,
Our laughter rings, a distant bell.
Memories dance like leaves in flight,
Fading softly into the night.

In the corners of a familiar room,
Lingering scents, a hint of bloom.
Time molds moments, shapes the past,
Echoes linger, shadows cast.

Through streets we wandered, hand in hand,
Marked by footprints in the sand.
Under the stars, a silent plea,
Your heart found home, next to me.

Yet seasons change, and winds will blow,
Tides of fate we cannot know.
Though paths may shift and drift apart,
Your echo rests within my heart.

The Touch of Tension

In the silence, we stand still,
Fractured air, a gnawing thrill.
Eyes locked tight, words left unsaid,
In this moment, both fear and dread.

A heartbeat races, time suspends,
Beneath the strain, a tension bends.
An unspoken truth beckons near,
Will you stay, or will you disappear?

Fingers tremble, the air ignites,
Crackling sparks in cold moonlight.
Do we surrender or break the chain?
In this dance of pleasure and pain.

Through thorny paths, we find our way,
A balance struck, come what may.
With every glance, the world could shatter,
Yet in this tension, hearts still chatter.

Intertwined Destinies

Paths that twist, a fateful thread,
Each step forward, our futures wed.
In gentle tides of time and chance,
We find our way, a destined dance.

Stars align, a cosmic play,
Underneath the vast array.
In every storm, in every sigh,
Together we rise, together we fly.

The universe whispers, secrets unfold,
Through whispered tales, our love is told.
With every heartbeat, every kiss,
We weave our dreams, a boundless bliss.

In the tapestry of fate we roam,
Two souls together, one shared home.
Intertwined worlds, neither lost nor found,
In love's embrace, forever bound.

Love's Silent Trade

In quiet moments, we exchange,
Silent promises, hearts arranged.
No need for words, just a glance,
In this quiet, we find our chance.

Glimmers shared, the light within,
A twinkling spark, where dreams begin.
With gentle touches, fate's embrace,
In love's trade, we hold our place.

Whispers linger, soft and low,
In tender spaces, trust will grow.
The art of giving, receiving grace,
In every heartbeat, our sacred space.

Through storms that pass, we'll stand side by side,
In the silent trade, where love won't hide.
In every moment, a treasure bestowed,
In this silent journey, our hearts behold.

Heartstrings and Hard Bargains

In the quiet of a bustling room,
We negotiate with words and gloom.
Each heartbeat weighs a heavy cost,
In love, we find what seems now lost.

Promises tied with fragile thread,
Whispers linger where fears are fed.
Though we barter with our hearts,
It's the price of love that ever imparts.

Time is fleeting, yet we hold tight,
In shadows casting soft moonlight.
Hearts tugging on the tethered line,
In every struggle, a trace of divine.

We dance around what we can't see,
Hard bargains forged in ecstasy.
Yet somewhere deep in fragile hearts,
A truth remains as the world departs.

The value lies in what we give,
In pushing back against how we live.
Heartstrings pulled with gentle grace,
We find our home in this embrace.

The Impact of Intimacy

In whispered tones, our secrets flow,
A gentle touch that stirs the soul.
In shared moments, we find our truth,
A sacred bond holds our lost youth.

Stars aligned, we breathe the same air,
Every hug erases depth of despair.
Intimacy blooms like flowers in spring,
A precious gift that love will bring.

In every glance, a story unfolds,
In silence, our hearts' language holds.
When hands intertwine, the world fades away,
And darkness retreats from the light of day.

Time cascades like a gentle stream,
Filled with echoes of every dream.
The impact lingering like morning dew,
In each heartbeat, a bond anew.

Through laughter shared and tears of woe,
We've built a bridge where few dare go.
Intimacy, our divine embrace,
Carries the weight of time and space.

The Power of Sweet Exchange

In laughter bright, our spirits rise,
With every word, a sweet surprise.
The power lies in what we share,
In simple gestures, love laid bare.

Exchanges made with heart and mind,
In every corner, we seek to find.
Connection sparkles in fleeting gaze,
In sweetness, the ordinary conveys.

Gifts wrapped tight with intention pure,
Moments shared, of that we're sure.
With every token, hearts do mend,
In the power of words, we transcend.

Each smile exchanged, a thread well spun,
Binding two souls to become as one.
In quiet spaces where silence sings,
The sweetest exchange is what love brings.

In simple realms where kindness grows,
The seed of connection ever sows.
In every embrace, we find the way,
To cherish the power of today.

Gravity of Togetherness

In every laugh, a tether tight,
Together we bask in soft moonlight.
With whispered dreams and open hearts,
In unity, the journey starts.

Through storms that rage and winds that howl,
We stand as one, a sacred vow.
Gravity pulls us near and true,
In every challenge, we break through.

Holding hands beneath the stars,
Mapping dreams, no distance far.
We weave our lives with care and grace,
Finding strength in our safe space.

In the dance of days, we're intertwined,
Each heartbeat echoes what we find.
Togetherness, our richest thread,
In love's embrace, we're surely led.

Through thick and thin, we face the test,
In tangled fates, we find our rest.
Gravity of love, unyielding force,
In togetherness, we steer our course.

The Fortunes of Forged Bonds

In shadows deep where trust is found,
Two souls entwined, their hearts are bound.
Through storms they stand, unbroken, strong,
Together they sing life's vibrant song.

With every laugh and whispered grace,
They carve their names in time and space.
Forged in the fires of trials faced,
A treasure grows, no love can waste.

In silence shared and solace given,
These bonds create a life worth living.
With every tear, they grow more wise,
A fortune found in love's true prize.

They weather seasons, calm and wild,
In every moment, love's a child.
Each promise made, a sacred thread,
In tapestry of life, they're wed.

So cherish this, the gift they weave,
For in their hearts, they truly believe.
The fortunes found in woven ties,
Are timeless treasures that never die.

Heartbeats as Currency

In quiet moments, whispers flow,
Heartbeats echo, soft and slow.
With every pulse, transactions made,
In love's rich bank, no debt can fade.

The laughter shared, a golden gain,
In every hug, they ease the pain.
Time spent together, wealth unmeasured,
Their bond becomes a priceless treasure.

Through gentle words and tender looks,
They weave their fate in sacred books.
Each heartbeat, like a coin once spent,
In love's great ledger, there's no lament.

They trade their hopes, their dreams, their fears,
In moments shared, through joy and tears.
The currency of trust will grow,
As hearts align, love's seeds they sow.

So count the beats, let none be lost,
In every heartbeat, love's true cost.
A fortune built on sharing space,
In vibrant hearts, a sacred place.

Alloyed with Affection

In hearts combined, a metal strong,
Alloyed with love, where we belong.
Each moment shared, a fusion bright,
Together shining, day and night.

In laughter's clang and silence soft,
They forge their bond, no fear aloft.
Through life's demands, they shape the clay,
With every touch, they're here to stay.

Their shared dreams form a sturdy beam,
Holding up hopes, a steadfast dream.
In trials faced, they bend, not break,
Strengthened together for love's own sake.

With each embrace, they meld as one,
Two hearts entwined beneath the sun.
Through heat and time, their essence gleams,
Alloyed with affection, they chase dreams.

So treasure this, the boundless flow,
For in their hearts, true riches grow.
An alloy strong, forever bright,
In love's embrace, they find their light.

The Gains of Affectionate Choices

In every choice, their hearts align,
Affection blooms, a sacred sign.
Through paths they walk, side by side,
In love's embrace, they shall abide.

With gentle hands, they shape their fate,
Each moment shared, a choice so great.
In laughter's ring and silence true,
Affection guides in all they do.

The gains they reap, not gold or fame,
But joy and trust, a vibrant flame.
In every hug, in every tear,
Their choices pave the way, so clear.

They weigh their words, each one a gem,
In bonds of love, they build their stem.
For in decisions, hearts will thrive,
Affectionate choices keep love alive.

So cherish these, the moments spent,
In choice and love, their souls are lent.
The gains of love, in life's embrace,
Are treasures found in every space.

Whispers of a Heart's Equation

In the quiet of the night, they speak,
Secrets tangled, tender and meek.
Every glance, a silent plea,
Yearning hearts in symphony.

Numbers dance on a faded page,
Each heartbeat marks a timeless stage.
With every breath, the truth unfolds,
A love story that never grows old.

Whispers linger in the air,
Promises wrapped in a gentle care.
Counting stars, we trade our sighs,
In this bond, nothing ever dies.

Equations formed, emotions blend,
A riddle penned that has no end.
In their eyes, reflections play,
A journey that guides our way.

Together, we calculate the night,
Finding solace in shared light.
Two souls bound by silent devotion,
A heart's equation, an endless ocean.

The Currency of Affection

In shadows cast by waning light,
Affection weighs, a gentle might.
Each smile shared, a coin we spend,
Treasures found in love's blend.

With every hug, we make a trade,
A market bustling, unafraid.
The warmth exchanged, worth more than gold,
Countless riches in stories told.

In tender whispers, words align,
Currency flows, pure and divine.
Every moment, a valued share,
An investment in the love we care.

Though distances may stretch so far,
Our hearts remain, a guiding star.
In laughter's echo, we define,
A wealth that grows, forever entwined.

So let us gather, rich and bold,
In the currency of hearts, behold.
The love we forge will never wane,
An everlasting, sweet refrain.

Bonds Beyond Measure

Two hearts entwined, a silent vow,
In this embrace, no need to bow.
Distance fades, our spirits soar,
A bond that holds forevermore.

Through storms we stand, hand in hand,
In unity, we make our stand.
Trust is forged like iron steel,
In every smile, a shared ideal.

Invisible threads, they intertwine,
Strong as forges, divine design.
In laughter's dance and sorrow's sigh,
We rise together, reaching high.

Measuring love by moments shared,
In every glance, it's love declared.
No scale could ever track the depth,
Of the promise held with every breath.

So here's to us, in the light we shine,
Bonds beyond measure, yours and mine.
Through all the trials, we'll remain,
Together forever, without a chain.

The Weight of Unspoken Promises

In the quietest of hours, they stay,
Unvoiced dreams linger and sway.
Each heartbeat echoes hopes untold,
A story wrapped in shadows bold.

Promises hang like stars in the sky,
Eclipsed by fears that pass us by.
With every glance, a secret shared,
In silence, our vulnerability bared.

Through whispered winds, intentions flow,
Carrying dreams that softly glow.
The weight we bear, both light and grave,
In each shared breath, courage we save.

Lost in the folds of a warm embrace,
We find solace in this sacred space.
Beneath the weight of words unsaid,
A deeper language, love's thread.

So let us treasure what is felt,
In the quiet, our hearts will melt.
For the weight of promises may remain,
Yet in our silence, love's refrain.

The Scale of Yearning

In shadows cast by twilight's glow,
A whisper stirs, a silent woe.
Each breath a wish, each sigh a plea,
A heart that longs, yet stays so free.

A distant star, a guiding light,
It calls to me through endless night.
Waves of longing, ebb and flow,
With every pulse, emotions grow.

In dreams of warmth, I seek your face,
Time stands still in our embrace.
The scale of longing, heavy still,
Yet I hold on, against my will.

Moments fleeting, like grains of sand,
Slipping through the open hand.
Yearning paints the sky in hues,
Of love's rich tapestry, we choose.

So here I stand, beneath the stars,
With hopes that echo distant bars.
In every heartbeat, watch it soar,
The scale of yearning asks for more.

Forces of Devotion

In the calm before the dawn,
A promise rests, a bond is drawn.
The pull of hearts, a gentle tide,
Together we stand, side by side.

Through storms of doubt, we find our way,
With every word, our truths display.
Devotion's force, a fiery spark,
Igniting hope within the dark.

We walk this path, our spirits blend,
In trust and love, we never bend.
With every step, we conquer fear,
The forces strong, our vision clear.

In laughter shared, in tears we shed,
The stories told, the words unsaid.
A bond that's forged in trials faced,
In forces true, our dreams embraced.

Through time's great weave, we journey on,
In shadows long, till light is drawn.
Together bound, let nothing shake,
In forces of devotion, hearts awake.

When Hearts Converge

In silence whispers softly blend,
As two souls meet, their journeys end.
When hearts converge, a magic blooms,
In gentle light, the darkness looms.

Frequencies of love, a sweet refrain,
Echoing softly, like summer rain.
In every glance, a universe shared,
When hearts converge, none are impaired.

The path of fate, like rivers flow,
Intertwined destinies, spirits glow.
Two voices rise, a melody pure,
In harmony found, we discover the cure.

Through every trial, hand in hand,
With trust and faith, together we stand.
When hearts converge, the world ignites,
In passionate flames, we reach new heights.

Let time unfold as dreams unfurl,
In the dance of love, we twirl and whirl.
When hearts converge, a truth we learn,
In unity's strength, forever we yearn.

A Tug of Hearts

The morning sun paints skies anew,
While thoughts of you pull me through.
A tug of hearts, a magnetic pull,
In every breath, this longing's full.

In laughter shared, and moments sweet,
A bond so strong, no chance to cheat.
Through waves of time, we drift and sway,
A tug of hearts, come what may.

With every glance, the world stands still,
A silent promise, a sacred thrill.
The heart speaks truths that words can't say,
In this sweet dance, we find our way.

Through every storm, and each delight,
In shadows cast by soft moonlight.
The tug of hearts, a force so bold,
In every story yet untold.

With every touch, the spark ignites,
Our souls entwined in endless flights.
A tug of hearts, where love resides,
Through every journey, side by side.

The Alchemy of Hearts

In whispers soft, our souls entwine,
With each beat, an echo, divine.
Crafting love from moments rare,
Transforming dreams in tender care.

Golden sparks in twilight's glow,
Two hearts dance, a seamless flow.
The essence of our sacred art,
Creating magic, heart to heart.

In laughter's grace, in sorrow's tears,
We forge our bond, dismissing fears.
Alchemy of joy and pain,
A masterpiece, love's sweet refrain.

Through storms we sail, through calm we glide,
Each trial faced, with you beside.
Together, we alight the night,
In love's embrace, forever bright.

Hand in hand, we chase the dawn,
With every breath, a new love born.
In this journey, hearts collide,
The alchemy of love our guide.

Shadows of Longing

In the quiet hours, shadows play,
Longing whispers, night turns to day.
Heartbeats echo, a silent plea,
Yearning for what's meant to be.

Beneath the stars, I trace your name,
A flickering flame, forever the same.
Lost in the dusk, too far to hold,
A story written, yet untold.

In every dream, your face appears,
A ghostly touch that soothes my fears.
Memories linger, like whispers faint,
A canvas painted, love's true saint.

Through the veil of midnight's sigh,
I reach for you, as time drifts by.
The shadows stretch, the longing grows,
In every heartbeat, love still flows.

Yet hope remains, a guiding star,
Even in distance, no matter how far.
Our souls may wander, but they shall meet,
In shadows' embrace, where hearts retreat.

The Kinetic Dance

In rhythm spun, our bodies sway,
A kinetic dance, lost in play.
Gravity bends with every glance,
Caught in the thrill of this wild dance.

Moments flash like stars at night,
We twirl and weave, pure delight.
Hands collide, a spark ignites,
Chasing dreams in silver lights.

Every step, a story told,
In the rhythm, our spirits bold.
The world fades, it's just us two,
In this dance, eternity's view.

With laughter ringing, the tempo climbs,
We move as one, in perfect rhymes.
The heartbeats sync, a song that plays,
In this kinetic waltz, we blaze.

As shadows stretch and sunlight bends,
We're lost in time, where the music ends.
In every spin, love's vibrant trance,
Forever caught in this grand dance.

Blossoms of Affection

In the garden where flowers bloom,
Blossoms whisper, dispelling gloom.
Petals soft, a touch divine,
Love unfurls in sweet design.

Every color, a story shared,
Fragrant dreams, tenderly paired.
Under sunlight, hearts ignite,
Dancing lightly, pure delight.

Seeds of hope in each embrace,
Growing stronger, a sacred space.
Through seasons change, we stand tall,
Blossoms of affection, through it all.

With every breeze, our joys extend,
Nature's tapestry, love to tend.
In life's cycle, we intertwine,
A garden nurtured, yours and mine.

So let us wander, hand in hand,
Through petals soft, across this land.
In every bloom, our love reflects,
Eternal blossoms, life connects.

The Push and Pull of Us

In the dance of hearts, we sway,
With every step, we drift away.
Yet, like tides that kiss the shore,
We're pulled back in, wanting more.

The tension builds, a silent scream,
A tangled web of hopes and dreams.
In shadows cast by love's own light,
We find our way, a spark ignites.

Through chaos, calm begins to weave,
A fragile thread that won't deceive.
Together, we falter and rise,
In this playground of sweet surprise.

When storms arise, we hold on tight,
Two souls entwined in endless fight.
The push and pull—our gravity,
In every glance, infinity.

Yet patience blooms, with time's embrace,
A patient smile upon your face.
Through every turn and twist we take,
We navigate the path we make.

Sway of Sentiment

Beneath the trees, shadows dance,
Whispers shared in chance romance.
Each sigh, a note in timeless rhymes,
A heartbeat's echo, love in chimes.

The breeze carries secrets untold,
In the sway of dusk, feelings unfold.
A fleeting glance, a knowing smile,
In this moment, we pause a while.

Crickets sing as stars ignite,
With tender words, we chase the night.
In every brush, soft sparks arise,
A universe within our eyes.

With every touch, the world fades wide,
In the warmth of you, I confide.
Emotion swirls in mystical flight,
Together we dance, hearts alight.

The sway of sentiment is real,
In every tremor, we can feel.
As night unfolds, we chase our dreams,
In newfound love, nothing's as it seems.

The Cost of Connection

In bridges built, a toll we face,
Every laugh, a moment's grace.
Yet shadows linger, fears do creep,
We gamble hearts, our secrets keep.

The weight of promise, heavy chain,
Each choice a slice of joy or pain.
The path we walk is fraught with scars,
Beneath the love, a world of wars.

A glimpse of truth can chill the bones,
In every fracture, silence moans.
Yet in this cost, a beauty blooms,
A daring heart that breaks the gloom.

Through every challenge, we emerge,
With deeper roots, our spirits surge.
The cost of connection—worth the strife,
For in your arms, I've found my life.

With tender hands, we mend the seams,
In the tapestry of shared dreams.
Together, we bear this heavy load,
In love's currency, we find our code.

Attraction's Equation

In the realm where souls collide,
A spark ignites, we cannot hide.
An unspoken law, a pull so true,
In every glance, I am drawn to you.

Chemistry brews in subtle touch,
Every heartbeat says so much.
Like waves that crash on shores untold,
Our bodies move as secrets unfold.

The math of hearts, a perfect score,
In your presence, I crave more.
Two figures dancing in the night,
An equation where everything's right.

With every laugh, a fraction grows,
In every whisper, the tension flows.
In this moment, we align,
A cosmic force so rare, divine.

As numbers rise and angles shift,
In our embrace, we find the gift.
Attraction's equation, simple yet grand,
In this infinite dance, we understand.

Hearts in the Balance

In shadows deep, where whispers play,
Two hearts collide, both lost and stray.
The scales they tip, with hopes confined,
Yet still they dance, in love entwined.

A fragile bond, it sways and bends,
With every breath, the tension mends.
Decisions loomed, like clouds above,
But trust prevails, a sign of love.

Through storms that rage, and winds that blow,
Their anchored souls, begin to grow.
In every trial, they find their strength,
Together forged, they'll go the length.

With every choice, the heartbeat pounds,
In silent vows, their truth resounds.
The balance holds, as fate unfolds,
A tale of love that time upholds.

The Weight of Affection

A heavy heart, yet light as air,
Each glance a weight, a silent prayer.
Emotion strains, like bending wire,
Yet pulls them close, igniting fire.

Through tender words, a bitter sweet,
They share the load, as souls compete.
A gentle touch, a fleeting glance,
In shared silence, their spirits dance.

Yet burdens rise, like tides that swell,
In sacred trust, they cast their spell.
With hands entwined, they face the night,
In darkened hours, they find the light.

Each heartbeat echoes, a rhythmic sound,
Within their chests, true love is found.
In every weight, they find their grace,
Together, strong, they'll find their place.

Affection's Finesse

In subtle glances, hearts will spar,
A graceful dance, that's who they are.
With tender words, like silk they weave,
A tapestry that won't deceive.

Through patient steps, they learn and grow,
With every breath, the feelings flow.
In every pause, the silence speaks,
A language rich, the heart it seeks.

With skillful care, they mold their fate,
In every moment, no rush, no hate.
An artful balance, both near and far,
A shining light, their guiding star.

With playful tease and gentle sighs,
Affection blooms, beneath the skies.
In every laugh, a spark ignites,
Their bond a dance, through day and nights.

Tipping the Scale of Desire

With every glance, desire calls,
Their hearts aligned, where passion sprawls.
An unspent thrill, a hidden fire,
Together drawn, they climb higher.

In whispered dreams, ambitions rise,
They chase the stars, where longing lies.
A fervent pulse, a tethered thread,
In woven hopes, their spirits spread.

The scale tipped right, to hearts on fire,
A potent mix of love and desire.
In every touch, the world grows still,
Fueled by the ocean of their will.

In every sigh, their souls align,
Each moment shared, a bottle of wine.
With every heartbeat, love ignites,
Tipping the scale, to endless heights.

The Symphony of Synergy

In gentle waves, we weave our art,
A dance of souls, an open heart.
Each note a bond, a shared embrace,
Together we find our rightful place.

Like stars that twinkle in the night,
We harmonize, our dreams take flight.
In unity, we craft our song,
A melody where we belong.

With every chord, our spirits soar,
A tapestry of evermore.
Each rhythm beats, a pulse so true,
In symphony, I laugh with you.

Our voices blend, a vibrant hue,
Through trials faced, we push on through.
In strength we find, in love we stand,
Together, we create, hand in hand.

The music swells, it fills the air,
An unseen force, beyond compare.
In synergy, we make our mark,
A lasting light, igniting spark.

Forces Unseen

In shadows cast, where whispers lie,
A strength resides, though we can't spy.
Like tides that shift with moon's command,
These forces guide, an unseen hand.

The pull of dreams, an urge to flow,
A current deep, where few will go.
Invisible threads, they shape our fate,
We feel their tug; we can't await.

The breath of life, a silent breeze,
In gentle ways, it aims to please.
Through spirit's touch, we rise above,
These forces weave the tale of love.

A cosmic dance, we twirl within,
The strength of bonds that never thin.
In every heart, a whisper stirs,
The unseen force, it softly stirs.

So trust the path, though blurred it seems,
For forces unseen guide our dreams.
In unity, we find our light,
Embrace the night, embrace the flight.

The Binding Thread

A silver line connects us all,
Through laughter, tears, we're free to call.
In shared moments, a sacred bind,
The thread unites, our hearts aligned.

With every story, the yarn grows tight,
Woven through time, in warmth and light.
Through trials faced and joy we share,
This binding thread, a whispered prayer.

Each knot we tie, a memory held,
In colors bright, our fears quelled.
A fabric strong, though weathered worn,
In love, our threads are truly born.

Through storms we stand, together brave,
This binding force, our hearts it saves.
The tapestry of life unfolds,
In every thread, a story told.

So cherish these connections dear,
For every thread, a bond sincere.
In unity, we are complete,
The binding thread beneath our feet.

Emotive Equilibrium

In tranquil seas, emotions sway,
A balance found in night and day.
With gentle tides, our hearts align,
In peaceful calm, our fears resign.

The dance of joy and sorrows deep,
In harmony, our spirits keep.
A state of grace, where we can be,
In flow with all, just you and me.

Each breath a pulse, in rhythm true,
In stillness found, our strength renew.
Through trials met and paths we roam,
In equilibrium, we find our home.

With colors bright, emotions blend,
In every heart, a message send.
To feel the weight, to learn to soar,
In balance, we can ask for more.

So let us sway, in tune with fate,
In every joy, in every weight.
For in this dance, we are alive,
Emotive equilibrium helps us thrive.

Threads of Unity

In a tapestry we weave, together we stand,
Strands of hope and joy, woven by hand.
Colors blend and dance, under the sun,
A masterpiece of hearts, united as one.

Each thread tells a story, of dreams that we share,
In laughter and whispers, in moments so rare.
Through trials we grow, stronger each day,
Bound by our spirit, come what may.

Hand in hand we journey, through thick and thin,
Embracing each other, letting love in.
With every knot tied, our bond is defined,
In this fabric of life, our souls intertwined.

Together we rise, like the sun in the sky,
Guiding each other, as time passes by.
These threads of our lives, silken and bright,
We cherish forever, a beautiful sight.

The Whispered Balance

Between the moonlight and the dawn's embrace,
A gentle whisper sings, soft as lace.
It dances on the breeze, so light and fair,
A balance of shadows, and light in the air.

In the hush of night, where secrets reside,
It cradles our thoughts, like a calm tide.
With each breath we take, harmony flows,
In the silence of peace, a garden grows.

The pulse of existence, a steady refrain,
In chaos and calm, it soothes all pain.
Finding the center, where opposites meet,
In this quiet dialogue, our hearts feel complete.

In every moment, we seek and we find,
The whispered balance, a path intertwined.
Guided by starlight, our spirits align,
In the dance of existence, a world divine.

A Canvas of Connection

Brush strokes of kindness, colors so bright,
On this canvas of life, we paint our own light.
With each vibrant hue, a story unfolds,
A tapestry woven, in shades of the bold.

Every heartbeat echoes, in rhythmic refrain,
A symphony played, like the softest of rain.
Together we create, a masterpiece grand,
In this gallery of dreams, hand in hand.

Splashes of laughter, drips of our tears,
Layered with memories, spanning the years.
Every stroke a moment, a bond we embrace,
In this canvas we share, our dreams find their place.

From cool shades of blue, to fire's warm glow,
The beauty of difference helps our love grow.
In every creation, our spirits connect,
A canvas of feelings, we lovingly reflect.

The Architecture of Emotion

In the heart's deep chamber, emotions reside,
A fortress of feelings, where passion won't hide.
With walls made of laughter, roofs made of tears,
We build our own stories, through joys and fears.

Each room holds a memory, each floor a dream,
In this grand design, we find our theme.
From the foundation of trust, we rise above,
Crafting a structure, built strong on love.

Windows wide open, letting the light in,
We gather the warmth, where our journeys begin.
Balconies reach out, to the world's vast expanse,
In the architecture of life, we dare to dance.

Our heart's design flows, in curves and in lines,
Each detail reflects, the love that intertwines.
With blueprints of hope, we sketch our way through,
In this building of dreams, it's me and it's you.

The Foundations of Cherished Alliances

Together we stand, hand in hand,
Building bridges, strong and grand.
Trust and laughter, woven tight,
Our bond shines through the darkest night.

In trials faced, we find our way,
Supporting each other, come what may.
Every moment, cherished anew,
In this alliance, truly, we grew.

With kindness planted, seeds of grace,
Our friendship blooms in every space.
Nurturing warmth, we share the load,
On this path together, we strode.

The echoes of joy, they fill the air,
In shared memories, love lays bare.
Each step forward, we grow as one,
Under the warmth of the golden sun.

Through seasons change, we stand so true,
In the heart's garden, friendships brew.
Together forever, we carve our fate,
The foundations laid, we celebrate.

The Pooling of Dreams

In whispered hopes, our dreams collide,
Each aspiration, a joy-filled ride.
Together we gather, visions vast,
In the stillness, we find our cast.

With open hearts, we share our fears,
Through the shadows, we wipe the tears.
Our futures woven, bright and clear,
In this union, we hold each dear.

Casting wishes upon the stars,
Mapping the journey of who we are.
With every heartbeat, our dreams take flight,
In the vast canvas, we paint the night.

Pooling our hopes is a sacred art,
Each longing embraces the other's heart.
In the blending of souls, dreams ignite,
Creating a tapestry, pure delight.

Together we climb, the summit we reach,
In unity's strength, we learn and teach.
With hands intertwined, our spirits soar,
In this dance of dreams, we crave for more.

Mutual Gains in the Garden of Hearts

In the garden where kindness grows,
We nurture love, as each flower shows.
With open arms, we plant and tend,
Harvesting joy with each true friend.

Together we water, roots intertwined,
In this sanctuary, our souls aligned.
Each smile shared brings blossoms near,
In precious moments, we hold dear.

As seasons change, we reap the yields,
With trust and grace, our bond shields.
In the shade of love, we find our place,
The harmony shared, our warm embrace.

In laughter's echo, we sow delight,
With every trial, we find the light.
Compassion blooms, both wild and free,
In this garden, the best of we.

As petals fall and new buds sprout,
We celebrate what friendship's about.
With hearts in bloom, we gain anew,
Together, forever, a vibrant hue.

The Symphony of Shared Riches

In harmony, our voices rise,
Creating melodies, breaking ties.
With laughter's notes and kindness' grace,
We weave together our warm embrace.

Each shared moment, a vibrant chord,
In the symphony, we find our reward.
Through highs and lows, we sing the tune,
In the light of friendship, we dance with the moon.

The treasures of love, we freely give,
In the music of life, together we live.
With every heartbeat, we play our part,
In this grand orchestra, the song of the heart.

With every note, our spirits soar,
Unified rhythms, we long for more.
In the richest refrain, we find our way,
Together in concert, come what may.

As encore echoes in twilight's glow,
The symphony shared continues to flow.
In the legacy built, we find our fame,
In the music of life, we're never the same.

Transactions of the Heart

In silence we trade whispered dreams,
Beneath the glow of soft moonbeams.
Promises linger in the air,
A currency found in love's rare fare.

Each glance shared, a quiet deal,
Brush of hands, a shared appeal.
We barter hope, we gamble trust,
In this transaction, love is a must.

Every moment, a little fee,
On the ledger of you and me.
Hearts exchange like precious art,
In these transactions of the heart.

Confessions penned in secret ink,
In every pause, we start to think.
The value grows with every sigh,
In the twilight where feelings lie.

So let us trade until the dawn,
In this marketplace, love's never gone.
For in each act, we find our part,
In the transactions of the heart.

Affection's Tipping Point

A gentle touch, a fleeting glance,
In the balance, we dare to dance.
Each heartbeat sways, a weighing scale,
Love teeters there, a fragile trail.

The tides of emotions rise and swell,
In this moment, all is well.
With laughter shared, hearts intertwine,
Revealing signs, a love divine.

A whisper shared, the world falls still,
In the warmth of a shared thrill.
Each secret kept, a bond increased,
In affection's grasp, we find our feast.

Words spilled like wine, sweet and bold,
In the light of dawn, our story told.
Cascading feelings, a vivid art,
At the precipice of the heart.

As moments linger, edges blur,
We reach the point where dreams occur.
In every touch, we paint our slate,
At affection's tipping point, we create.

A Bargain of Bliss

In twilight's glow, we weave a spell,
As laughter rings like a distant bell.
We exchange glances, a sweet delight,
In this bargain, everything feels right.

With every promise, a paper thin,
A fragile pact where love begins.
Hearts entwined through every choice,
In whispers soft, we find our voice.

Together we barter dreams untold,
In the warmth of arms that hold.
Tender moments crafted, rare,
In this bargain of bliss we share.

In shared silence, we draw the line,
In stolen moments that feel divine.
We risk it all for love's sweet kiss,
In the threads of fate, we find our bliss.

So seal this deal with heart and soul,
Together, we feel completely whole.
For life's a trade, where joy resides,
In this bargain of bliss, love abides.

The Balance of Emotion

In every heartbeat, a weight unfolds,
Silent stories waiting to be told.
Joy and sorrow dance in time,
In the balance where love does climb.

With every smile, a subtle cost,
In the clash of feelings, never lost.
We navigate the highs and lows,
In the garden where affection grows.

Through laughter shared, we find our ground,
In the sweetness of love, we're bound.
Every tear, a lesson learned,
In the fires of passion, we're eternally burned.

Emotions weigh, yet lift us high,
In the tethered dance, we fly.
With every moment, finely spun,
It's the balance of emotion, two become one.

So let us walk this line of fate,
In each heartbeat, we choose our state.
For love's embrace keeps us sincere,
In the balance of emotion, we persevere.

Worth in Whispers

In quiet moments, worth is found,
Whispers echo, soft and profound.
Value whispered in gentle sighs,
Treasures hidden where silence lies.

Amidst the noise, a soft refrain,
Nurtures the heart, eases the pain.
In stillness, worth begins to bloom,
Filling the ever-darkening room.

Each word, a jewel, precious and rare,
Draws forth the beauty, we often share.
In whispers, truths of love unfold,
A story written, quietly told.

Beneath the rush, a heartbeat slows,
In whispered love, our essence grows.
Moments cherished, softly embraced,
In quietude, our worth is traced.

So listen close, to what is near,
In subtle whispers, we draw near.
For worth is found in gentle breath,
A promise lived, not bound by death.

Affinity's Gravitational Pull

In the dance of eyes that meet,
An unspoken bond, so sweet.
Magnetic hearts, drawn to ignite,
A force unseen, a shared light.

Like stars that twinkle in the night,
We navigate through love's pure fright.
In every smile, a silent call,
Affinity pulls us, can't resist at all.

Through laughter shared and tender gaze,
We lose ourselves in this soft haze.
In moments wrapped, we linger long,
Caught in the rhythm of our song.

Unfolding paths, we venture near,
Each step together, shedding fear.
A journey's start, endlessly drawn,
Awakening thoughts, love's new dawn.

So let us dance, the universe wide,
In affinity's pull, forever abide.
For in this force, we find our way,
Bound in love, come what may.

The Price of Devotion

Devotion's weight is never light,
A costly gift, it takes its flight.
Through trials faced, our hearts lay bare,
In sacrifice, we show we care.

The silent tears shed in the night,
More than mere words that take to flight.
Each moment spent, a currency,
Invested deeply, endlessly.

In acts of love, we find the toll,
A journey deep into the soul.
For passion's fire can burn too bright,
Transforming darkness into light.

Still, through the struggle, grace appears,
With every heartbeat, calm our fears.
In truth, the price we gladly pay,
Gains riches found in every day.

Devotion whispers, soft and true,
Binding us tightly, me and you.
In every breath, through joy and pain,
The price of love, our greatest gain.

The Leverage of Tenderness

In tender moments, strength resides,
Through gentle touch, our heart abides.
Soft-spoken words can heal the soul,
A simple gesture, making us whole.

With each embrace, the world seems right,
In vulnerability, we find our light.
The leverage held in every glance,
A silent pact, a sacred dance.

When storms arise and shadows creep,
It's tenderness that helps us keep
Our hearts aligned, the path made clear,
In love's warm glow, we have no fear.

The power lies in hands entwined,
In every heartbeat, love's reminded.
Through trials faced, together we stand,
Anchored tightly by tender hands.

So let the world rage on outside,
In tenderness, we choose to abide.
For in this strength, we rise above,
With the leverage found in love.

Weaving Tides

In the dance of the ocean's embrace,
Waves whisper secrets, a silent grace.
Colors merge in a fluid blend,
Time drifts gently, tides never end.

Stars blink above in the night sky,
Carried by winds that softly sigh.
Moonlight kisses each crest so bright,
Weaving dreams in the canvas of night.

Depths hold treasures, shadows sway,
An unseen story in every spray.
Lovers lost in the sea's warm hold,
Their fates intertwined, forever bold.

Currents tug at the heart's vast sea,
A journey shared, just you and me.
Fleeting moments, like shells on sand,
Gathering echoes, hand in hand.

As dawn breaks with bursts of gold,
A promise of new tales to be told.
With each wave, memories rise and fall,
Together we stand, answering the call.

The Pulse of Passion

In the firelight, shadows twist and turn,
Hearts ignite with an aching burn.
Words like embers, soft and sweet,
With every heartbeat, our souls meet.

Electric whispers dance on skin,
A world awakens, where dreams begin.
Eyes that shimmer like stars at night,
In silence, we find our shared light.

Moments linger, time feels slow,
In this warmth, our feelings grow.
Two hearts beating, a steady sound,
Lost in each other, we're unbound.

Passion flows like a river deep,
In the darkest hours, secrets keep.
Every glance, every sigh,
A testament to love that won't die.

With every dawn, the world anew,
We chase our dreams, just me and you.
The pulse of passion, fierce and bright,
Guides our way through day and night.

Shadows and Light

In the stillness of the evening air,
Shadows linger, mysteries laid bare.
Light cascades through the trees above,
Whispers of nature, echoes of love.

Illuminated paths twist and turn,
Through dappled glades, our hearts discern.
Every flicker tells a tale untold,
Of courage found and fears left bold.

As day gives way to dusk's embrace,
We find reflections in time and space.
Chasing dreams where shadows meet,
In this dance of light, we are complete.

Beneath the stars, the night's soft glow,
Trust the journey, let feelings flow.
For in the darkness, there's hope to find,
In every shadow, love is kind.

With each new dawn, the light will rise,
Bringing warmth to our fragile ties.
Together we'll walk, in heart and mind,
In the dance of shadows, love is blind.

The Crux of Together

In the heart of unity, we stand strong,
A melody echoing, a timeless song.
With hands entwined, we navigate,
The winding path that love creates.

Moments shared, laughter fills the air,
Every heartbeat, a promise we share.
Through trials faced, we hold the light,
Guiding each other through darkest night.

A tapestry woven with threads of gold,
Stories exchanged, both new and old.
In the warmth of togetherness found,
We rise like phoenixes from the ground.

As seasons change and years unfold,
In every chapter, our love stays bold.
Together we journey, side by side,
Our hearts as anchors, our dreams as guide.

In the crux of together, we're never apart,
Two souls united, one beating heart.
With every sunrise, our bond grows tight,
We are the stars, forever igniting light.

Anchored in Desire

In the depths where dreams reside,
Waves of longing crash and glide.
Silent prayers to skies above,
Footprints mark the dance of love.

Tides may pull, yet we hold fast,
Heartbeats echo, shadows cast.
With each pulse, our spirits soar,
Anchored in what we adore.

Stars align in midnight's glare,
Whispers soft, a soothing prayer.
Through the storm, we find our way,
Together, forever we stay.

Fires burn in amber light,
Illuminating endless night.
In this haven, hearts find peace,
From longing's grip, we seek release.

In every glance, desire's flame,
Fueling a never-ending game.
With every touch, the world feels right,
Anchored in this love's delight.

The Power of Embrace

In the stillness, warmth we find,
A sanctuary built from time.
Where words fade and silence speaks,
In your arms, my spirit seeks.

Gentle sighs beneath the stars,
Healing wounds, no longer scars.
Every heartbeat, blended sound,
In this closeness, love is found.

Time suspends, the world erased,
Moments linger, softly traced.
Wrapped in tenderness, we feel,
The power of this love is real.

Two souls weaving, soft and bright,
Guided by the moon's soft light.
With every hug, the universe sighs,
In the embrace, the world complies.

Beneath the weight of dawn's first glow,
Still we hold, still we know.
In this bond, we find our grace,
Together, lost in time's embrace.

Weighty Whispers

Softly spoken in the dark,
Secrets shared, igniting spark.
In the hush, a tender plea,
Weighty whispers, just for me.

Eyes that dance with unvoiced dreams,
Carrying all that silence seems.
Every glance, a story told,
Mapping paths where hearts unfold.

Breathless moments linger on,
Silent echoes find their song.
Holding truths that fear might shun,
Weighty whispers, two as one.

In the stillness, shadows play,
Guiding lovers on their way.
In this trust, the bold confess,
Weighty whispers bring them rest.

Through the night and into dawn,
All our doubts are gently drawn.
In the quiet, hearts are free,
Weighty whispers, you and me.

Hearts Entwined

In the garden where we meet,
Petals fall beneath our feet.
With every laugh, roots grow deep,
Hearts entwined, no need for sleep.

Tender glances, soft as air,
Moments stretch; we feel the care.
Like the vine that clings to oak,
In this bond, love's words are spoke.

With each heartbeat, rhythms blend,
Promises that will never end.
Hand in hand through life's parade,
Hearts entwined, unafraid.

Seasons change, yet we remain,
Weathering all, joy and pain.
Through the storms, our light won't wane,
In this love, we feel no chain.

If the world should tear apart,
You will always be my heart.
In every shadow, I will find,
Forever yours, our hearts entwined.

Embracing the Pendulum

In shadows cast, it swings so wide,
A rhythm found, we must abide.
With every tick, a heartbeat shared,
In timeless dance, we feel prepared.

The pull and push, like tides at sea,
A balance sought, just you and me.
In cycles deep, we rise and fall,
Together strong, we conquer all.

Each swing unveils a brand new day,
With open hearts, we find our way.
As moments bring their sweet embrace,
We lose ourselves in time and space.

In quietude, we hear the song,
The pendulum, it won't be long.
As time resets its gentle sweep,
In every swing, our trust we keep.

So here we stand, aligned and true,
Embracing all that we pursue.
For in this dance of ebb and flow,
We find the love that makes us grow.

The Dynamics of Desire

In gentle whispers, passions rise,
Two hearts collide beneath the skies.
With every glance, a spark ignites,
Desires unfold like moonlit nights.

Each breath we take ignites the flame,
In this wild game, we stake our claim.
The pull of you, a magnetic force,
Guiding me through this fervent course.

In shadows deep, we chase the thrill,
With fervor found, we lose our will.
An ardent dance, a whirlwind tight,
Our bodies sway in pure delight.

With every kiss, a promise made,
In passion's grip, we won't evade.
The dynamics shift, a tender play,
In longing's reach, we find our way.

So let us dive into the flame,
In this sweet longing, find our name.
For in desire's embrace, we soar,
In every heartbeat, we crave for more.

Harmonics of Affection

In every note, a love's refrain,
A symphony where hearts remain.
With melodies that softly blend,
In harmonics, all wounds we'll mend.

Together singing through the night,
Each whisper pulls, a sweet delight.
With rhythms rich, our souls entwined,
In every chord, our fate defined.

The music swells, a rising tide,
With you beside, I feel alive.
Each echo speaks of love's embrace,
In perfect time, we find our place.

Through every challenge, every strife,
Our song endures, a cherished life.
With every heartbeat, every sigh,
In harmonics pure, we rise and fly.

So let us play this grand duet,
With every note, I won't regret.
For in the symphony we share,
We weave a tapestry so rare.

A Gentle Pull

In stillness, I feel your gentle pull,
A quiet strength, a heart so full.
With every touch, the world can fade,
In sacred space, our bond is made.

Like drifting leaves upon the breeze,
Your presence soothes, my mind's at ease.
In tender moments, passions grow,
The depth of love begins to show.

With every heartbeat, soft and true,
I am forever drawn to you.
A soothing force, an anchor strong,
In your embrace, I know I belong.

Through every storm, your light will guide,
A gentle pull, forever side by side.
With every sunrise, anew we'll find,
In love's sweet grasp, our hearts aligned.

So here we stand, in warmth and grace,
With every moment, we embrace.
For in this pull, we walk as one,
A journey shared, our lives begun.

Captive Currents

In a river of dreams, we swim slow,
Caught in whispers of the ebb and flow.
Each ripple speaks of hidden tales,
Of love that brews as the current sails.

Beneath the surface, secrets dwell,
Encased in shadows, where feelings swell.
We navigate the depths in disguise,
Dancing with fate beneath the skies.

Through currents fierce, we find our way,
Guided by stars that gently sway.
The pulse of nature beats as one,
And in this tide, we are never done.

A journey forged in water's embrace,
Every swirl, a familiar trace.
Captive to magic, fragile yet bold,
In this fluid world, our tales unfold.

Together we flow, through joy and strife,
Captured in the current, we share this life.
No chains can bind what the heart has found,
For in this ocean, true love is crowned.

The Synergy of Souls

Two spirits dancing in cosmic light,
Merging energies that feel so right.
Silent harmonies hum in the air,
A bond unseen, yet intricately rare.

In the laughter shared and the tears we bare,
Each moment glimmers, a sacred flare.
Like stars aligning in the night sky,
Together we soar, never asking why.

Your heartbeat echoes, a drum in my chest,
In the rhythm of life, we find our rest.
Every glance, a spark that ignites,
Illuminating truths on shadowy nights.

With every word, we weave our fate,
In this tapestry, we elevate.
Like water and earth, we blend and grow,
In the synergy of souls, love's vibrant glow.

Through trials faced and mountains climbed,
In partnership, our hearts are chimed.
Unbreakable threads that time can't sever,
Together we thrive, now and forever.

Melodies of Togetherness

In harmony's embrace, we sing our song,
Every note unfolds, where we belong.
A symphony of laughter, love, and dreams,
Interwoven stories, flowing in streams.

The piano whispers secrets of the heart,
While strumming guitars play their part.
With every refrain, a moment's grace,
Together we dance in this sacred space.

Echoes of joy ripple through the air,
As melodies rise, banishing despair.
In soft serenades, our spirits blend,
Creating a magic that will never end.

The chorus of life, rich and profound,
In the symphonic journey, love is found.
Through crescendos bold and softest sighs,
Together we flourish, as time flies.

With instruments played and hearts entwined,
In the music of love, true peace we find.
Melodies linger, forever they stay,
In the rhythm of togetherness, come what may.

The Gravity of Connection

In the pull of your gaze, I feel it near,
An unspoken bond, crystal clear.
Like moons drawn close in celestial dance,
In the gravity of connection, we take a chance.

Threads of fate pull us, silently tight,
Binding our spirits, day and night.
Through distances measured, we never part,
For your essence resides within my heart.

Every heartbeat echoes the love we weave,
A tapestry rich, in which we believe.
With every embrace, the world feels right,
We shine together, a beacon of light.

In laughter that sparkles, in tears that flow,
Our souls entwined, forever to grow.
Invisible ties that no one can break,
In the gravity of love, we never quake.

In moments of silence, we still understand,
Feeling the pulse of a guiding hand.
As stars collide and fate connects,
In this dance of life, our hearts reflect.

Convergence of Whispers

In the stillness, voices blend,
Secrets shared, hearts extend.
The echoes dance in twilight's haze,
Creating bonds in soft arrays.

A gentle breeze, a tender sigh,
Words on lips, like stars on high.
Each murmur weaves a tapestry,
Of dreams and hopes, a symphony.

The shadows speak in quiet tones,
Reminding us we are not alone.
In every whisper, love is found,
An endless rhythm, a sacred sound.

As night enfolds the wandering light,
Whispers linger, spirits ignite.
In every heart, a story spun,
The convergence shared by everyone.

Together we stand, a silent crowd,
In whispered thoughts, we are allowed.
The world may spin, but here we stay,
Holding each whisper, come what may.

The Fluidity of Feelings

Like rivers flow, emotions shift,
Through valleys deep, our hearts uplift.
Each swell and fall, a shifting tide,
In the dance of life, we take our ride.

A flash of joy, a shadowed tear,
The waves of life pull us near.
In every heartbeat, passion thrives,
In the fluid embrace, our spirit strives.

Transient joys, like morning dew,
Fleeting moments, fresh and new.
Each pulse a testament, raw and real,
In this vast ocean, we learn to feel.

Together we navigate the streams,
Chasing after forgotten dreams.
Every ripple whispers in our ears,
The fluidity reflects our fears.

With open hearts, we face the flow,
Unraveling treasures only we know.
In this dance of endless emotion,
We find our place in the vast ocean.

Embers of Unity

In the twilight, sparks ignite,
Embers glowing, hearts take flight.
Together we gather, a radiant fire,
In the warmth of souls, we never tire.

A flicker of hope in the darkest night,
Burning bright, a guiding light.
Each spark a promise, a bond untold,
Fanning the flames, our stories unfold.

In moments shared, we spark the glow,
Through trials faced, together we grow.
Unity embraces with gentle might,
Stoking the embers, igniting the night.

Every laugh, every tear we share,
Weaving a tapestry beyond compare.
In the heat of our passion, we find our way,
Embers of unity, here to stay.

For in this circle, we stand as one,
With hearts ablaze, we've just begun.
In harmony's glow, we'll light the path,
A dance of embers, igniting the wrath.

The Currents of Togetherness

Through gentle tides, we drift as one,
In currents strong, the journey's begun.
Each wave a whisper, a soft embrace,
Carrying dreams through time and space.

With hearts aligned in rhythmic flow,
We navigate the highs and lows.
In every turn, we find our way,
The currents guide us day by day.

Together we rise, together we fall,
In the ocean of life, we heed the call.
As waters merge, our souls entwine,
In the currents of love, we brightly shine.

With every tide, our spirits soar,
In the dance of life, we seek and explore.
Through gentle sway, we find our truth,
The currents of togetherness, eternal proof.

So let us sail on this sea divine,
Through tempests wild and sun that shines.
In the embrace of waves, we discover bliss,
Together forever, sealed with a kiss.

The Underlying Pulse

In the silence, shadows weave,
A rhythm felt, beneath the leaves.
Each heartbeat thuds, a guiding force,
A quiet strength, in nature's course.

Through the thicket, whispers flow,
Barefoot steps on earth below.
Life embraces, gently binds,
The pulse of love in every find.

Mountains rise, rivers bend,
A timeless dance that won't end.
Stars ignite the velvet night,
In their glow, we find our light.

When the storm clouds gather near,
The pulse persists, calming fear.
With every breath, the world confirms,
In hidden places, life still churns.

Through seasons change, we learn to trust,
The pulse endures, a sacred must.
It whispers softly, wild and free,
In every heart, the harmony.

Sweet Oppositions

Daylight dances on the sea,
While shadows play a melody.
Joy and sorrow intertwine,
In every sip of love's sweet wine.

Fire warms the chilly air,
While the moonlight casts a stare.
With passion strong, and gentle grace,
Two worlds meet, in time and space.

A storm can break the still of night,
Yet in the dark, there's glimmers bright.
Laughter's echo, sorrow's song,
In opposites, we all belong.

Waves crash loud, then softly sigh,
Beneath the stars, the wishes fly.
Love's embrace, fierce yet mild,
In every heart, forever wild.

Day and night in sweet refrain,
Together, they embrace the pain.
A tender pulse of heartbeats blend,
In this dance, we transcend.

The Tug of Heartstrings

A gentle pull, a quiet plea,
Heartstrings tug, a symphony.
Through whispers soft and calls that rise,
Connection forms beneath the skies.

Each moment shared, a tender thread,
In every laugh, in words unsaid.
A dance of souls, entwined so sweet,
With every step, our hearts repeat.

Distance stretches, but binds us tight,
A lighthouse glimmers through the night.
With open arms, love crosses space,
In every heartbeat, our embrace.

Melodies woven with care and grace,
In the raw rhythm, we find our place.
With every glance, the world aligned,
In the tug of heartstrings, we are blind.

Time may fade, but love remains,
In memories bright, and soft refrains.
Through trials faced, we grow strong,
The tug of heartstrings, where we belong.

Chains of Warmth

Linked together, hand in hand,
In this warmth, we understand.
Beneath the weight of earth and sky,
Love's chain is forged, we cannot lie.

Through winter's chill, we find our glow,
In laughter shared, against the snow.
With every hug, a bond we make,
Chains of warmth, that life can't shake.

Storms may come, and doubt may rise,
Yet anchored firm, we share our ties.
With every tear, we cleanse the past,
Chains of warmth, a love that lasts.

In shadows cast, we seek the light,
Against the darkness, we ignite.
Through trials faced, our spirits blend,
Chains of warmth, a love to mend.

With open hearts, we dare to dream,
In every smile, a radiant beam.
Together strong, we boldly stand,
In chains of warmth, forever planned.

Reflections of Synchronicity

In quiet moments, we align,
Two hearts dancing, fate entwined.
Glimmers of truth in the night,
A spark ignites, a shared light.

Whispers of destiny's call,
In harmony, we rise and fall.
Fragments of time, softly blend,
A journey where paths will mend.

Every glance carries a tale,
Winds of fortune, we set sail.
In the mirror of the soul,
Together, we become whole.

Moments weave our sacred thread,
Past shadows, where dreams are fed.
In synchronicity, we trust,
Through tears and laughter, we must.

A cosmic dance, a woven fate,
Hand in hand, we navigate.
In this life, we intertwine,
A tapestry, divine design.

Bonds Beyond Measure

Like roots that ground a timeless tree,
Our bond runs deep, wild and free.
Through storms and sun, we stand tall,
In whispered secrets, we share all.

With every hug, with every word,
In silence too, our hearts are heard.
A thread unbroken, pure and true,
Together, there's nothing we can't do.

In laughter's warmth, in sorrow's shade,
In every moment, love is made.
An endless trust, a sacred space,
In this embrace, we find our place.

Though miles may stretch and time may bend,
Our souls connect, our spirits blend.
Bonds crafted by both joy and pain,
In every loss, there's love to gain.

Through every trial, we'll endure,
A love that's fierce, unwavering, pure.
Together we rise, together we fall,
In this great tapestry, we are all.

The Poise of Togetherness

In unity, we find our grace,
A gentle hand, a warm embrace.
Steps aligned, we move as one,
In the daylight, in the sun.

With every laugh, a bond does grow,
In shared moments, we come to know.
The strength of hearts that blend as two,
In our reflection, we find the view.

Through storms we weather, hand in hand,
In quiet strength, together we stand.
A circle strong, with love as glue,
In harmony, we will pursue.

Each story told, a thread we weave,
In joys and sorrows, we believe.
With every heartbeat, a pulse we share,
Together's power, beyond compare.

In the stillness, a promise made,
In understanding, fears will fade.
In this journey, side by side,
The poise of togetherness, our guide.

Echoes in Harmony

In distant hills, our voices soar,
Echoes linger, forevermore.
Two melodies entwined as one,
In every heart, our song is spun.

With every beat, our spirits rise,
Underneath the same vast skies.
Notes of laughter, whispers of dreams,
In life's great dance, nothing is as it seems.

Our footprints trace the sands of time,
In sync with rhythms, pure and prime.
A chorus of hopes, softly sung,
A language understood by the young.

Through trials faced and victories won,
The echoes linger, never done.
In harmony, we learn to trust,
Through every challenge, rise we must.

As stars align, our pathways glow,
In every joy, our spirits flow.
Echoes in harmony, we sing,
Together forever, love's sweet ring.

In the Presence of Without Measure

In quiet rooms, shadows play,
Silence speaks in a gentle sway.
Time drips like honey, sweet and slow,
Moments linger, soft and low.

Whispers dance like a cool breeze,
Filling hearts with tranquil ease.
Here love finds its sacred space,
Each breath shared, a warm embrace.

Waves of warmth pulse through the air,
In this haven, we lay bare.
Emotions stretch, like clouds above,
In the presence of endless love.

Stars align in a velvet night,
Guiding dreams with their soft light.
Each heartbeat echoes soft and clear,
In the presence, you are near.

Eternal is this sacred bond,
In your gaze, I feel enthroned.
Together, we soar, our spirits free,
In the presence, we always be.

A Spectrum of Heart's Inflation

Colors bloom in vibrant dance,
Each hue whispers a sweet chance.
Hearts expand like the morning sun,
In this spectrum, we are one.

Laughter rings like silver bells,
Every note a tale that dwells.
Vibrations pulse, the world ignites,
In this spectrum, joy takes flight.

Shadows float in a gentle sway,
Painting love in shades of gray.
Yet hope arises from the dark,
A spectrum blended, every mark.

Moments flash like fireworks bright,
Illuminating the velvet night.
Each heartbeat paves the way to grace,
In this spectrum, we find our place.

Together, we weave a story told,
In colors rich, in threads of gold.
A palette vast, our spirits soar,
In this spectrum, forevermore.

The Architecture of Affectionate Deals

In the chambers of trust, we build,
Foundations strong, our hearts fulfilled.
Drawing lines with gentle hands,
In love's design, together we stand.

Each promise laid, a brick in time,
Crafting dreams in rhythm and rhyme.
Windows wide to let light flow,
Within these walls, our feelings grow.

Blueprints drawn with laughter's trace,
Every inch, a cherished space.
In the architecture, we find our song,
Creating a world where we belong.

Through storms, we fortify our ground,
Amidst the noise, love's voice resound.
A fortress built on shared ideals,
In this craft, affection reveals.

Through corridors of time we roam,
In every corner, we find home.
The architecture stands so tall,
In affectionate deals, we have it all.

The Potential of Connected Souls

In the depths of silence, we ignite,
Two souls merging, shining bright.
In every glance, worlds collide,
In the potential, we abide.

Threads of fate weave through the dark,
Binding our hearts, igniting spark.
In the stillness, we learn to trust,
Life's symphony, in love we must.

Each heartbeat echoes a shared song,
In this dance, we both belong.
The universe bows to our will,
As connected souls, we are still.

Echoes of laughter flood the night,
In every tear, we find the light.
Together, we soar, unconfined,
In the potential, love defined.

In dreams, we find the paths to tread,
In every thought, the love we've bred.
Connected in ways the heart knows,
In this bond, our spirits grow.

Milton Keynes UK
Ingram Content Group UK Ltd.
UKHW021935121124
451129UK00007B/99